FABULOUS HAIR

FABULOUS HAIR

Written by Maria Neuman
Photography by Angela Coppola

DK

LONDON, NEW YORK, MUNICH,
MELBOURNE, AND DELHI

Editor Elizabeth Hester
Designer Jee Chang
Managing Art Editor Michelle Baxter
Art Director Dirk Kaufman
Publishing Director Beth Sutinis
Lead Illustrator Jeremy Canceko
Additional Illustrations Matt Dicke,
Paul Hoppe, Engly Cheng, Erin Harney
Production Ivor Parker
DTP Design Kathy Farias

DOWNTOWN
BOOKWORKS INC.

Produced by Downtown Bookworks Inc.
President: Julie Merberg
Director: Patty Brown
Editor: Sarah Parvis

Photographer Angela Coppola
Freelance Beauty Editor JoanneNoel Higgins

First published in the United States in 2006 by
DK Publishing, Inc.
375 Hudson Street
New York, New York 10014
06 07 08 09 10 10 9 8 7 6 5 4 3 2 1

Library of Congress Cataloging-in-Publication Data

Neuman, Maria.
  fabulous hair / written by Maria Neuman. -- 1st American ed.
    p. cm.
  Includes index.
  ISBN 0-7566-1589-5 (pbk.)
  1. Ornamental hairwork--Juvenile literature. 2. Hairstyles--
Juvenile
literature. 3. Braids (Hairdressing)--Juvenile literature.   I. Title.
TT976.N48 2006
646.7'24--dc22

          2005031580

Color reproduction by Colourscan, Singapore
Printed and bound in Mexico by
R. R. Donnelley and Sons Co.

Discover more at
www.dk.com

contents

What's Your Haircare IQ?

Hairstyles for School

Hairstyles for the Weekend

Party-Time Hair!

Alexis

What is your haircare IQ?

Just like your face or your feet, your hair is unique to you. In this book, we're here to show you that no matter what length, texture, or type your hair is, there are lots of cool styles out there that are right for you—from a quick updo before gym class to a funky bun for the mall or a glam-o-rama French twist for a fancy party. As well as creating exciting styles, you'll learn to take care of your locks and keep them looking their best. With some simple steps and key products, this will be a breeze. So, are you ready for some serious hair education? Need to know the difference between gel and mousse? How to make that updo work for you or the secrets to accessorizing with pizzazz? *Fabulous Hair* has you covered!

What is your hair type?

Before you can start styling up a storm, it's helpful to figure out exactly what type of hair you have. It can make a huge difference in how a style looks on you, as well as what type of styling products you should use. Check out the pictures and descriptions of the girls on these pages, and match yourself to the one (or ones) who looks most like you. Then watch out for her picture throughout the book—she'll have specialized style tips just for you!

how to use this book

style tip
If you've got bangs, just twist them back in Step 2 and secure them with a couple of bobby pins above your ears.

Watch out for these tip boxes throughout the book—the girls will have some great tips for every hair type.

These symbols at the beginning of each style will give you an idea of how much time that style will take to create.

Hair pro or beginner? One white bar means a style is easy; four means it's pretty tricky. Take your pick.

Alexis

Hi, I'm Alexis! If your hair is long, medium-thick, and straight like mine, you probably have many of the same issues as I do, like...

• My hair can sometimes look flat and stringy.

• I can curl my hair with hot rollers, but it won't stay in place unless I use some styling products.

• My hair can look oily if I don't wash it everyday.

• My hair gets funny flyaways in dry weather.

• Any type of volumizing product like mousse or gel looks great in my hair.

Nikki

My name is Nikki. I love my dark hair color and great shine. I have fine hair but it can look thick because I have a lot of it. Fine hair can be tricky to style because it just wants to lie flat. Is this you?

• Even a ponytail can look wimpy with my fine hair.

• Even with gel and curlers, my style will only last a few hours.

• I need lots of hair spray to keep an updo in place.

• I like to wash my hair every day—otherwise it will look really flat and greasy.

• Light products like gel and mousse work on my hair, but heavier stuff like creams and pomades just weigh it down.

Rosie

Amy

Nierah

My name is Rosie. All my friends say they wish they had my curls, but this hair can drive me crazy! Do you go through this?

- My hair gets frizzy in the rain or humidity.

- With any sleek style I need to straighten my hair first.

- My hair can only be kept under control with lots of leave-in conditioner and straightening cream.

- Pomades and waxes are great for separating my hair.

- I don't need to wash my hair every day, because it's a bit dry.

I'm Amy. My hair is thick and a little bit wavy, and I've got long bangs. I like my hair just hanging down, but sometimes it's a little tricky in an updo. Is this you?

- If it's humid outside, my hair gets frizzy.

- A curling iron works great on my hair as long as I use gel before and spray after.

- Since my hair is thick, I can skip a day of shampooing because it never looks flat.

- If I start blow-drying my hair when it's too wet it will take forever. Slightly damp works best.

- My hair gets flyaways when the weather is dry and cold.

My name is Nierah. Short hair like mine can be fun and easy but it can also be limiting. My hair is coarse, which makes it perfect for updos because it stays in place well. Does this sound like you?

- My hair is great at holding a curl, but since it's dry I have to be careful using a curling iron or any other heated styling gadgets.

- I can skip the shampoo a couple of days in a row but I always need to condition my dry ends.

- Light products like gel and mousse are drying on my hair. I need leave-in conditioners, styling creams, and pomades.

- My hair can get flyaways when the weather is very dry.

Found your hair-type partner?
Time to style!

stylingstuff

Hair is beautiful naturally, but making it look great in a style takes a little help from the right products. Remember this rule of thumb: The finer your hair, the lighter your products should be. Fine-haired girls should stick to a misting of light hair spray or a puff of mousse. Thick or curly hair can take a heavier pomade or gel. No matter what type you choose, be careful not to overdo it—the only way to take product out is to hit the showers! Read on to see how to achieve your style goals.

clean and condition

shampoo, conditioner,
leave-in conditioner

If your hair is oily, wash it every day. Girls with curls usually have drier hair, so you can easily skip a day. Shampoo right down to your roots—but avoid putting too much conditioner right on your scalp as it can make hair look limp.

smooth and straighten

pomade, wax, shine spray

If you're plugging in a straightening iron, make sure to spritz each section of hair with a straightening spray to keep it protected. Waxes and pomades add a messy, piece-y edge to all styles but should only be used sparingly.

how much?

To avoid looking frizzy or over-slicked, be sure to use the right amount.

A pea-sized amount of product is good for heavy stuff like pomades and waxes.

A quarter-sized amount is great for leave-in conditioner, styling cream, or gel.

A tennis ball–sized amount is right for fluffy stuff like mousse.

Listen up, fine-haired females: mousse works great on damp hair and should be applied from roots to ends. A volumizing gel should just go on the roots because it's a little thicker.

volumize
mousse, gel

hold
gel, hair spray

Everyone needs a good hair spray. If you're creating an updo, it's always the final touch. A quick spray over the whole head will keep everything in place.

tool school

The number one trick to creating all of the hairstyles in
this book is to have the right tools. Not quite sure what
gadget does what? We've rounded up the most common
items (and the ones you'll need to do the looks in here)
and explained what each one does and any tips you need
to know when buying your own.

hot stuff

These are the stylers that dry, straighten,
or crimp your hair. They can get seriously
hot, so always use them with care.

A crimping iron has two
interlocking zigzag plates. To
use it, squeeze a section of hair
between the two plates for about
five seconds, then move down the
hair shaft.

A curling iron is the
fastest way to add curl. Choose
a wider barrel for a looser curl or
a narrow one for ringlets. Whatever
size you choose, only let hair set
about five seconds at a time.

A good blowdryer
makes drying time faster
and also helps lessen frizz.
Look for one that has both
hot and cold settings and a
nozzle attachment to direct the
air and downplay frizz.

A diffuser attachment
disperses air so it doesn't come
out of the blowdryer in one huge
blast (making curls a tangled mess).

Velcro rollers are
another way to get curls.
They have Velcro teeth to
grip hair and stay in place,
but you need a blowdryer
to heat and dry the hair.

Hot rollers are best
when you want princess-like
curls all over your head. They need
about 10 minutes to preheat and are
secured onto your head with special pins.

A flatiron gets hair stick straight. It's
made of two metal or ceramic plates
that work just like irons. To use, clamp
the flatiron at the top of a section
of hair. Then drag the flatiron down
the hair to the ends.

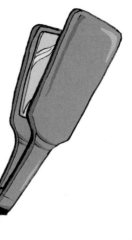

brushes and combs

Not only do brushes and combs get the tangles out, they are also the perfect styling partners for heat stylers or products.

A wide-tooth comb is best for combing wet or damp hair to get the tangles out. These are also good for combing through gel or mousse products evenly.

A round brush is what you need for blow-drying hair straight. The brush goes under a section of hair, pulling down from below while a blowdryer heats from above. It can also be used to curl ends.

A paddle brush has a flat surface with bristles popping out. It's best for brushing dry hair.

A fine-tooth comb is great for making a part in your hair and also for smoothing down a style when you're finished—a spritz of hairspray and a light combing with this tool will leave your style perfect.

pins and clips

No style will stay put without an array of pins, clips, and elastics. Trust us, you can never have too many.

Bobby pins are great for securing loose pieces to a tricky updo or pulling strands back from your face. Just open it up between fingers and slip it in. **A hairpin** is already open, and is better for fastening sections of a bun or twist into place.

bobby pin   hairpin

Jawclips come in small or large sizes. Just pinch the back pieces together to open them up and then clamp them down over the hair. The big ones can hold a ponytail, but the small ones are best for decoration or holding tiny twists of hair.

Hair elastics are fantastic. If you have fine hair, choose smaller ones; thicker hair can handle the chunkier styles. Elastics come in lots of sizes and styles, so be sure to pick the right one for your 'do.

10 tips for really **healthy hair**

Strong, shiny hair is the best foundation for any style. To keep your tresses looking their best, you need to learn how to care for your scalp and hair. That means nourishing, protecting, and grooming your locks. Be good to your hair, and it will love you back!

1

Get regular trims: Even if you're growing your hair, get it snipped every 3–6 months to keep the ends from splitting.

2

Lather up: If your hair is oily, wash it every day. If your hair is on the dryer side, feel free to skip a day.

3

Water works: If you're a pool queen, always rinse your hair with water after swimming to get rid of chlorine, which can fry hair and make blond locks look green.

4

Detangling tricks: Always use a wide-tooth comb to detangle your hair right after a shower.

5

Elastic alert: Don't use regular rubber bands to put your hair up. Use snag-free hair elastics to avoid breaks and split ends.

6

Food for thought: Your hair is a reflection of what you eat, so make sure to keep it looking good by eating lots of fruit, veggies, and lean protein (chicken and fish).

7

Product pick: You should only use two styling products at one time. If you need more to keep a style in place, it's probably not the right 'do for you.

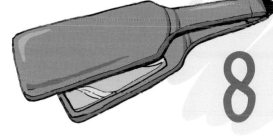

8

Hot hot hot: If you're unsure, ask a stylist to show you how to use a straightening or curling iron. If used incorrectly they can seriously fry your style.

9

Hey, sunshine! Hair gets sunburned just like your skin. Comb a dollop of sunscreen or leave-in conditioner through before you go to the beach.

10

Frizz factor: One of the main causes of frizz is rubbing wet hair with a towel to get it dry. Instead, just blot or squeeze it using a towel.

top-10 hair basics

The type of hairstyle you wear depends on what type of hair accessory you use. For example, a butterfly jawclip gives a totally different vibe than a flowery barrette. This is where you can really show your flair for fashion and keep your style in place. Below, we've rounded up 10 favorite hair treats, as well as tips for what to do with them and who they're best for.

1

Headbands are great for keeping hair off the face or spicing up a low ponytail.

2

Hairpins are great for securing a bun in place. With added blooms, they're pure pretty.

3

Bobby pins can decorate and hold your hair in place at the same time—genius!

4

Clips are cute to hold back growing-out bangs. Why not get some with attached ribbons in your school colors?

5

Chopsticks can hold a bun in place on their own, or just stick into a finished updo for a little Asian flavor.

6

Snag-free elastics are safe for hair because they don't have any metal joints. Plus, you can mix and match the colors to go with your outfit.

7

Skinny elastic headbands are great for pulling your hair off your face in class. They look cool just wrapped around your wrist, too.

8

Jawclips are perfect for keeping twists or braids from unraveling. Bigger versions can hold a whole ponytail in place. Just snap one on right at the scalp for a quick grip.

9

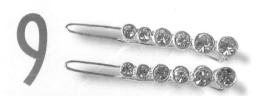

Baby barrettes are the perfect decoration for a fancy updo or when you just want to add some sparkle to your hair.

10

Combs like this are the hair-accessory equivalent of tucking your hair behind your ears. They work best on thicker hair.

Alexis

Nierah

Rosie

How do you wear your hair to school?

You know the drill: The alarm goes off and it's time to pull yourself together for another school day. It's a no-brainer to look for a fresh outfit every day, but hair can be a little trickier. Do you ever feel stuck in a style rut and end up just throwing your hair back into the same old ponytail? You're not alone. But there is help! The following pages are full of schoolday styles that can be created in minutes. You'll find enough variety to whip up new looks all week, and they're all PE tested and won't fall in your face during that crucial math test. So check out these super-cute 'dos, find your favorites, and get styling! You'll look so great from the neck up that no one would notice even if you *were* wearing the same duds two days in a row.

ziggityzaggity

Here's a quick and cool way to make your hair look funky even when it's just hanging loose. With a couple of quick turns of a comb it's simple to turn your basic center part into this jagged look. This is the perfect style to try if you've only got a few minutes before catching the school bus, because you can create the Ziggity Zaggity lickety split!

how to do it

you'll need: wide-tooth comb • hair spray

1 Start by combing damp hair using a wide-tooth comb. Comb hair forward, so the sides fall in your face.

2 Take the comb and, starting from the back of your head (right at the crown, where your natural parts starts), drag the comb forward in a diagonal line about one inch (2–3 cm). Separate hair with your hands as you go.

3 Switch to the opposite diagonal direction and go one inch (2–3 cm) that way. Continue switching back and forth until you reach the front of your head.

zigzag style alert

OK, now that you've mastered the Ziggity Zaggity part, it's time to do something with the rest of your hair. To really showcase that part, pick a style that sits low (like a ponytail, pigtail, or bun), and smooth hair back to give the part center stage.

change it up!

dress it up!

These clips prove that it's hip to be square!

A flowery bobby pin helps finish your smooth look in the prettiest way.

Decorative twists give this look a playful spin when they're placed at the corners of the part.

style tip

If you have fine hair, spritz on shine spray or leave-in conditioner to tame flyaways and keep your zigzag part looking clean and crisp.

A butterfly elastic is a pretty addition to any pony, and the bright yellow color draws attention to simple styles.

messypony

This is an easy way to make your favorite style a little funkier. The best part is that since it's supposed to be less than perfect, it's one of the few 'dos that's hard to do "wrong"! It actually works better on hair that isn't squeaky clean, so try this on a day when you haven't washed your hair, or as an easy updo after a busy day.

how to do it

you'll need: blowdryer • hair elastic • pomade

1 Start with damp hair. Flip your head upside down and blow-dry while scrunching up sections with your hands. Don't brush, as this will take away the messy effect. When it's dry, flip hair back and use your fingers to smooth it down.

2 Grab hair with both hands and pull it back into a loose ponytail. Use an elastic to fasten. The best place for your ponytail is right in the middle of your head, in the back.

3 Rub a pea-sized amount of pomade in your hands. Next, grab sections of your ponytail and massage the pomade into them one section at a time to create even more of a crazy, messy, cool look.

curly girls

If you're blessed with beautiful ringlets, place your pony a little lower and looser for a romantic look. The looser your ponytail, the more your curls will show—try placing the hair elastic in a few different locations until you find the one you like.

dress it up!

A beaded elastic has more drama than your average ponytail holder—but works just the same.

Decorative pins can transform a messy pony into an elegant 'do for special occasions.

A row of mini jawclips adds an extra accent.

Flowing ribbons fit the casual, romantic mood of a low, loose ponytail.

style tip

A bit of mousse can help plump up fine hair to get the fullness and body that look great in this style.

loopedpigtails

Feeling a little loopy? Then this style is perfect for you! These simple pigtails have been turned up and tucked under. Not only is this style a cinch to do, but it can also look super-cute and dressy if you just add the right accessory. If you're keeping it casual, we think it's great for keeping hair out of your face in gym class, too!

how to do it

you'll need: brush • comb • 2 hair elastics

1   Brush hair so it's knot-free. The use the end of a comb to divide it down the middle.

2   Gather one side into a pigtail and start securing it with an elastic. On the final wrap of the elastic, simply stop short of pulling the pigtail all the way through.

3   When you've got both pigtails looped, adjust them with your hands so that they are the same size.

style tip

If your hair is short and some parts sprout out of the pigtails, just go with it. It still looks totally cute.

making the braid

If your hair is crazy-curly, these pigtails will just look like two big hair poufs on either side of your head. To keep it sleek, put hair into pigtails, braid it, and secure with an elastic at the bottom. Then bend the braid under and pin it so the end meets the base.

Hide the ends of your hair under a big ribbon or choose one that's already attached to an elastic.

dress it up!

Cool textured elastics are a great way to add some color.

A shimmery flower elastic makes this funky style look dressed up.

Pale pink coral barrettes are a sweet way to pin back bangs or stray pieces.

baby twists

For a sweet style that's simple to do, these skinny twists can't be beat. This hairdo looks just as cute from the front as from the back, and looks pretty on all types of hair. Short-haired girls can make it work just by clipping twists a bit higher on the head. Got long layers? Try using this style as a fresh way to keep hair out of your face for school days.

how to do it

you'll need: hairbrush • comb • elastic

1 Brush your hair so that it is knot-free. Give yourself a straight center part using the end of a comb.

2 Take two small one-inch (2–3 cm) square sections from the front of your head (either side of your center part). Divide each section into two pieces and tightly cross one section over the other section until you reach the end. Secure with an elastic.

3 Join the two pieces at the back of your head with one elastic (take out the ones holding the two twists secure).

dress it up!

A shimmery clip clamps flat over hair and comes in pretty shades like iridescent pink.

This barrette can be worn with the metal part tucked under hair so only the flower shows. Cute!

Polka-dot jawclips are cool for school days and casual weekends, too.

Clip a barrette in to keep twists in place.

twisty chick

If you're feeling really creative, try doing four twists instead of two. Just follow the original steps except for Step 2, where you will take four sections instead of two. To keep it simple, do the two original twists first (Step 3) and then add the second pair.

style tip
Trying to grow out your bangs? This is the perfect style for you.

knotty**girls**

Not only is this one of our favorite school styles (it's funky and functional), but once you master knots, you can add them to a bunch of different styles. Think of it like tying a knot in a piece of string. Also, if you've got a shorter 'do, this style is adaptable—so now you and your best friend can sport the same style but still have it look totally different!

how to do it

you'll need: comb • gel • 3 hair elastics

1 Using the end of a comb, divide the front of your hair into three sections (left side, top, and right side). Rub a tiny bit of gel between your hands and smooth your hands over the sections of hair. Secure each section at the base, by your scalp, with a small elastic.

2 Grab one section and twist it around into a coil. Next, take the coil, tie it into a knot, and then push the knot down until it is around the elastic.

3 Coil and knot other sections the same way. Brush the rest of your hair and let it hang down.

short-haired knots

Shorter hair can be hard to tie into this style. To imitate the look without getting crazy-looking sprouts, try making knots or twists with smaller sections of hair. Try a bunch of small knots above the forehead or line up some twists along the side of your head.

dress it up!

A hard plastic flower is a fitting end for vine-like twists.

Add a Hawaiian punch with a hibiscus bobby pin.

These twist-in gems will add sparkle right next to the knots.

Matching pink bobby pins and elastics? Totally cute.

style tip

If your hair is curly, it's easier to create these knots while your hair is still damp to avoid tangles.

funkypigtails

Put a funky twist on a simple style. Whether you're walking the halls or walking the mall, this look is sweet and simple. We love it because it's easy to alter and is the perfect way to show off all your favorite colors with lots of elastics. (Add as many as you want—you can never have too many.) A perfect combination of cool and colorful!

how to do it

you'll need: wide-tooth comb • 6 hair elastics

1 Start by combing out damp hair using a wide-tooth comb. Next, take the end of the comb and make a center part. Secure both sections with elastics into two low pigtails.

2 Grab another pair of elastics and secure one onto each pigtail about halfway down.

3 Attach two more elastics, one on either end of each pigtail.

add a braid

For a special twist on this funky style, braid the hair between the elastics. You can loop the last section to add even more interest. It's a pretty way to keep your hair out of the way for sports and to stay super-cool on summer days.

change it up!

These hip elastics have pretty beading.

dress it up!

Chunky elastics like these are best for girls with thick or curly hair.

style tip

Girls with short hair can move the elastics closer together or use two instead of three.

Even skinny elastics can make a statement in bold colors and stripes.

sportypony

Need to look athletic and stylish at the same time? This is the look for you. It pulls all of your hair off your face and neck, so it's perfect for any sport from gymnastics to track. Also, check out our way of showing off your school colors by adding coordinating accessories. If you're on a team, show everyone this style so you can all take the lead in the style game!

how to do it

you'll need: wide-tooth comb • elastics

1 Detangle damp hair using a wide-tooth comb (this will help this style to look really smooth and sleek). Then, gather the hair from the top and side of your head and secure with an elastic just below the crown of your head.

style tip

If you want to use decorative ponytail holders on top of plain elastics, remember to add them as you go.

2 Gather about another third of your hair, pulling from the sides and the area just below the first ponytail. Secure with an elastic about two inches (5 cm) above your hairline.

dress it up!

A flower accent makes this style less sporty and more pretty.

Faux-suede elastics make the most of this style. Pick colors that contrast with your hair to make them stand out.

3 Now gather up all the hair and secure it into a low ponytail. Girls with longer hair can add another ponytail holder lower down, like the Funky Pigtail.

Large jawclips can stand in for hair elastics—or top off simpler ponytail holders to finish your look.

lowbraids

We love the look of braids, and being able to make a braid opens up all sorts of hairstyle possibilities! Since this look is all about casual, keep your accessories the same— skip the rhinestones and think flowers or shells, or try wrapping a bandanna around your head instead.

how to do it

you'll need: blowdryer • hairbrush • comb • 2 elastics

1 Prep hair by mussing it with your fingers, using a blowdryer to be sure hair is completely dry. Brush to de-tangle dry hair. Next, use the end of a comb to divide hair along a center part. Put one side into a loose pigtail to get it out of the way.

2 Carefully divide the loose side into three sections. Begin braiding by crossing the righthand piece over the middle piece, then the lefthand piece over the middle piece. Repeat until you reach the end of the pigtail, then secure with an elastic.

3 Now take the second side out of the pigtail and repeat Step 2 to make another braid. Once both braids are done, adjust the ponytail holders to be sure they look even. You're done!

style tip

If your hair is too short to stay neatly tucked into braids, pin the loose pieces back with a clip or bobby pin—or let the pieces fall for a style that's messy-chic.

dress it up!

This hair elastic will add a little petal power to the end of any braid.

A bright ribbon brings this look some girlish charm. Use two of the same color or mix and match.

A woolly hat tops this look in wintertime. The braids are smooth enough to fit under a fitted cap, and look adorable sticking out the bottom.

braidcrazy

One of the coolest things about this style is that you can do it the night before, and then clip in some accessories in the morning. (Tiny braids can be time consuming, so this isn't the look to try if you're running for the bus.) Also, once you've spent the time to do these tiny plaits, they'll last for a couple of days, so you'll have built-in style! Just change the accessories to keep it fresh.

style tip

Curly girls might want to apply a dab of straightening balm to each section before braiding to keep it sleek. Just put a tiny dab (the size of your pinkie nail) on your hands and apply the cream from the roots down to the ends.

how to do it
you'll need: hairbrush • small hair elastics

1 Brush hair so that it is knot-free. Take small one-inch square sections of hair (make about five) and secure them loosely with elastics. It's a good idea to pull the rest of your hair into a loose ponytail to get it out of the way while you're braiding.

dress it up!

A tiny butterfly jawclip will hold your plaits in place.

Mini jawclips can hold a few braids together.

Use a flowery clip to hold braids in a bunch.

2 Take the elastic out of one piece of hair and divide the piece into three sections. Begin braiding by crossing the righthand section over the middle section and then the lefthand section over the middle section. Repeat until you reach the end of your hair and secure with an elastic.

3 Braid the rest of the sections of hair around your face, then take the back of your hair out of the ponytail and give it one last brush.

Use a tiny clip to gather braids for a more polished look.

change it up!

simple sophistication

To change this style from fun to finished: Instead of keeping all the braids at the front of your head, distribute them along your part and then gather the mini-braids at the side of your head

ropebraid

OK, so you know how to do a basic braid. Are you ready to kick it up a notch? Try the rope braid. It's actually easier than a regular plait because hair is only divided into two sections instead of three. Also, we give you two different ways to wear the Rope Braid here—but why not try your own ideas? Do as many as you want and see how you like it.

how to do it

you'll need: hairbrush • 2 elastics

1 Brush dry hair back into a ponytail and secure with an elastic.

2 Separate the ponytail into two equal sections.

3 Tightly cross one section over the other section until you reach the end of your pony and secure with an elastic.

the baby rope

How cute is this? Instead of a regular braid at the side of your face, why not mix it up every once in a while with a mini Rope Braid. Secure it with a cute elastic or clip and you're good to go.

change it up!

A twisty elastic mimics the texture of the braid. Cool!

style tip

If you've got bangs, try the Baby Rope a little farther back. It will look just right coming from the hair right behind your bangs.

dress it up!

Put coordinating scrunchies at the top and bottom of the braid for some casual color.

These elastics are covered in beads. So pretty!

Hair gems look great in the Rope Braid. Just place them along the creases.

chicchignon

Whatever your plans for day and night, this cool twist is what you need. This is the type of style that looks cool all day—then, with a couple of tweaks and added accessories, it can easily be ready to party. That means you don't have to spend an hour in the mirror trying to create your 'do—and you can use all that extra time planning the perfect outfit instead!

how to do it

you'll need: 2 elastics • hair spray • bobby pins • shine spray

1 Gather dry hair into a ponytail at the back of your head. Make sure the top and sides look really smooth and sleek.

style tip

If your hair is on the shorter side, create this style while hair is a tiny bit damp. Massage a quarter-size dab of gel into the hair by starting with your roots and working your gel coated hands down to the ends. Now you can comb hair back and start with Step 1.

2 Spritz the ponytail with hair spray, then twist it until it's tight and begins to coil. Wrap the twisted ponytail around the elastic. Tuck the end of the ponytail under the bun and pin it in place with a bobby pin.

3 Pin the rest of the bun in place by grabbing hair from your scalp and the bun at the same time (this will make it feel budge-proof). Spritz your whole head lightly with a shine spray to make it look very glossy and glam.

dress it up!

This tortoiseshell piece can be secured over the bun for a whole new look.

Hair combs look great stuck on either side of the bun (so the teeth go into the bun) for a little added drama.

A hair pin with a giant flower is the perfect partytime addition to the Chic Chignon.

Rosie

Nierah

Amy

Nikki

Alexis

How do you wear your hair on the weekend?

Time to ditch your school books and get ready to have some good times. What are you doing this weekend? Going to the mall with your friends, seeing the newest blockbuster, having a sleepover, or just chilling out with your family? We know weekends are all about F-U-N—and we've got some cool 'dos that will suit the mood no matter what's on your calendar. You'll find ideas for every hair type as well as easy-to-follow tips on working a bandanna, mastering pretty hair jewels, and the newest flower hair accessories. Why not get your friends together and test a couple of these hairstyles on each other? Be sure to have some supplies on hand: pins, barrettes, ribbons, and lots of imagination!

pickapigtail

Pigtails might be super-simple, but that doesn't mean they have to be boring. Check out these cool ideas for adding a little pizzazz to a favorite style. Are you feeling a little hippie? Add a bandanna. Go girly by placing pigtails high on your head. Whatever you choose, be sure to add some personality to this funky style to make it truly your own.

how to do it
you'll need: comb • 2 elastics

1 Start by combing out damp hair using a wide-tooth comb. Next, take the end of the comb and make a middle part.

2 Brush one section of hair into a low pigtail, securing it behind your ear with a hair elastic. Do the same on the other side.

3 Finish the look by knotting a bandanna under the pigtails. You can match the bandanna to the elastics or mix it up—it's up to you!

dress it up!

With this cute cap, hat head is a very good thing.

This pretty ribbon is small enough to be subtle, but packs a color punch.

style tip

Bangs can do a disappearing act in this style—or take center stage. Let them hang normally for a funky vibe, or move the bandanna up to hold them back and out of sight

A ring of flowers draws extra attention to pretty pigtails.

A pink plastic bow tops this nifty elastic.

change it up!

aim high!

If you're more of a girly girl, skip the scarf and place your pigtails super high. Secure them with your favorite pink accessory for an added feminine touch. This style also looks super-cute if you have curly hair.

toptwist

 Have you always wanted to be a twisty chick? Well, now is your chance. This fun style is not only functional (it gets your hair out of your face), it's also funky and perfect for a day out with your friends. The number of twists you do is up to you—just use our ideas as a suggestion. It's easy to do fewer if your time is crunched.

how to do it

you'll need: wide-tooth comb • 3 medium jawclips • at least 6 mini jawclips • hair spray

1 Start by combing damp hair with a wide-tooth comb. When it's knot-free, comb all the hair straight backward from your forehead—this will make it easier to part.

2 Use your comb to divide hair into left-side, top, and right-side sections, securing each piece with a jawclip to keep hair separated.

3 Remove clip from one section and, at the hairline, select about half of that section to work with. Start twisting hair backward with your fingers, picking up more hair the further back you go. After a few inches, use a mini jawclip to secure the twist.

4 Repeat Step 3 until you've replaced all three big jawclips with two or three little twists each. Line up the mini jawclips so they're all in a row, then spritz your head lightly with hair spray and pat down any stray hairs.

dress it up!

Use bobby pins instead of clips for a different look. They can criss-cross or line up to look like a headband.

Pick jawclips in a bunch of cool colors and patterns.

With colorful elastics, you can wear the back of your hair in a ponytail instead of down. Match them up to the clips and you'll look totally together.

style tip

If your hair doesn't like to lie smooth, rub a quarter-sized dollop of gel through damp hair before you start twisting.

flirtyflick

This style gives the classic blow-out a kick. With the sides smooth and sleek, it's a great way to show off pretty hair ornaments—or you can wear it loose. It takes some styling stuff to keep this 'do all day, but even if the "flick" part falls, your locks should keep the polished look.

how to do it

you'll need: gel • wide-tooth comb • 6 large jawclips • blowdryer • round brush • flatiron

1 Start with damp hair. Massage a quarter-sized dollop of gel from roots to ends. Comb hair to remove tangles, then use the comb to make a side part from the crown of your head and forward. Divide hair into six sections (three top and three bottom), twisting and clamping each section with a jawclip.

2 Section by section, begin blow-drying hair straight. Use a round brush on the underside of the section, pulling hair down from roots to tips with the hairdryer blowing right above it. Keep hair taut. Repeat this until section is smooth, then move onto the next section.

3 Now for the "flick": Spritz ends with hair spray. When your flatiron is hot, clamp it a few inches above the bottom of your hair, flip it up (away from hair), and drag it to the ends. Continue flicking as many sections as you like.

dress it up!

Add these star clips on the side to add a bit of shine.

Star-spangled bobby pins clip hair back with a sparkly accent.

Hair gems look great attached right next to your part.

These shell bobby pins will look beachy keen clipping up your flicks.

style tip

To all you curly girls, it's totally possible to get your hair poker straight but it takes time—the curlier the hair the longer you will have to repeat Step 2.

so cute!

Flicks are adorable on shorter hair because they look a bit retro (think 1950's). Try them with a middle part and use a little shine spray so hair really gleams.

pigtailtwist

When it comes to hairstyles, this pigtail twist combines a bunch of them. It's got pigtails, braids, and a cool twisted bun, all in a funky style that looks amazing, especially on long and thick hair. It's also a perfect example of what can happen when you get creative. Wrap up this style with some pretty blooms, and your inner flower girl can really blossom!

change it up!

double up!

Instead of creating one braid in each pigtail, make a couple of separate ones. When you loop the braids around the base, make sure to leave the ends of the braid sticking out for an extra-funky edge.

how to do it

you'll need: paddle brush • comb
• 2 elastics • bobby pins

1 Brush out dry hair to get rid of tangles. Using a comb, create a center part from the front of your forehead all the way back to the bottom of your hairline. Secure each section in a low ponytail right behind your ear.

2 Divide each pigtail into three sections and braid. (Follow the steps on page 34 for creating basic braids.)

3 On each side, wind the braid around the base of the ponytail to make a bun. Tuck ends underneath, then secure the braid by pushing bobby pins through the braid and toward the scalp and center of the bun.

dress it up!

This orchld hairpin will hold any twist in pretty place.

Tiny rhinestones give this bobby pin a princess edge.

This dragonfly bobby pin keeps stray hairs from taking flight.

style tip

If you want the ends to stick out, add a dab of pomade to make them sprout perfectly.

theband

Whether your hair is long or short, slipping in a colorful headband always looks good (it's also great for keeping those growing-out bangs out of your face). The style we've created here is all about blow-drying your hair straight so your band can really stand out. Remember, this is not the time to be shy with color—be bold, bright, and beautiful.

how to do it

you'll need: straightening balm • wide-tooth comb • 6 large jawclips • blowdryer • round brush • shine spray

1 Rub your hands together and distribute the balm throughout your hair, starting at the roots and working your way down to the ends. Comb your hair to remove tangles, then use the comb to divide your hair into six sections (three top and three bottom), twisting and clamping each section with a jawclip.

2 Section by section, begin blow-drying your hair straight. Use a round brush on the underside of the section, pulling it down from roots to tips with the hairdryer blowing right above it. Keep your hair taut. Repeat this until the section is smooth, then move onto the next section.

3 Mist your hair with shine spray and brush out. Slide in your headband in a smooth motion. For a cute pouf at the front, just push the headband forward a little after it's placed.

dress it up!

This classic tortoiseshell headband has small teeth to keep your hair in place.

These fun, colorful elastic headbands look great if you wear a couple at a time.

style tip

Headbands look just as cute with curls. Just be sure to use shine spray or gel so frizz won't distract from this sophisticated style.

more band ideas

Don't think that you're limited to headbands. Experiment with bandannas, your favorite ribbon, or even a strip of an old T-shirt. Got a long scarf? Try using it as a headband and tying it around hair to make a ponytail. Now there's an accessory that's twice as nice!

A retro scarf will always look cool!

pool pigtails

On your marks, get set, go! If you're at a pool party and about to take the plunge, don't forget to put up your hair in this water-friendly style. Not only do these 'dos keep your hair out of your face during a game of Marco Polo, the leave-in conditioner will also stop your style from getting seriously dried out from the chlorine.

how to do it

you'll need: leave-in conditioner
• wide-tooth comb • 4 hair elastics

1 Spritz damp hair with a leave-in conditioner spray. Brush out using a wide-tooth comb and create a center part that goes all the way from your forehead to the nape of your neck, so that hair is divided in two.

2 Take the right side of your hair and comb it again so it's really smooth. Secure it with an elastic into a high pigtail. Do the same with the other side.

3 Gently twist one pigtail until it begins to coil. Make a loose knot, pulling the end of the pigtail through the loop. Secure with an elastic and repeat on the other side.

4 Give ends a tug so they sprout out the top, and you're ready to make a splash!

dress it up!

This plastic flower on an elastic is perfectly waterproof.

A mix of colored elastics gives a bold look.

Clips with rhinestones will make you a mermaid beauty.

A terry-textured elastic is pool-perfect.

switch it up

This variation is especially great for girls with longer hair: Just add braids to your pigtails before twisting, and you've got a cool style that will go over swimmingly!

style tip

After swimming, remember to rinse your hair with regular water to flush out the chlorine.

prettyplaits

You already know that braids are the bomb, but when you add a dash of color they become even cooler. Preparing for this style can be a creative activity in itself as you pick out your favorite ribbons. You'll want to try this style again and again as you find new colors and textures. You can even try a bunch of different colored ribbons at the same time for one very festive head!

style tip

If your hair is short, only make the braids as long as you can before hair starts sprouting out. A braid that only goes half way down the hair will still look great.

how to do it

you'll need: brush • hair elastic • ribbon

1 Start with dry hair and brush it to remove tangles. Grab a one-inch– (2–3 cm–) square section of hair from the front and secure it with a tiny elastic a couple of inches (about 5 cm) down from the roots. Now take a thin ribbon that is twice as long as your hair and tie it around the elastic, so that equal lengths are hanging down on either side.

2 Instead of dividing hair into three sections to braid, use the whole pigtail as one section, and the ends of ribbon as the second and third sections. Start braiding by crossing one ribbon over hair to center, then the other ribbon over to center, then the hair to center. Keep doing this until you reach the bottom of your hair.

3 Secure the end of the braid (hair and ribbons together) with another tiny elastic. Then wrap the ribbon around either side of the elastic to cover it up, and finish with a cute bow. Do as many of these pretty plaits as you want.

dress it up!

Add in these clips at the top of the braids for another ribbon detail.

Tiny jawclips can also help to secure the bottom of the braid.

These sparkly clips glisten while they work.

Pick a ribbon that's really bright—and don't forget to match it with your outfit!

half-curly/half-straight

Can't make up your mind whether to go curly or play it straight? How about half and half? The best thing about this style is that it doesn't matter whether you start with hair that's curly or straight—or anywhere in between—because the end result is a cool mix of both. Plus, depending on what kind of accessories you pick, this semi-updo can go from a casual afternoon to a party without a hitch!

how to do it

you'll need: gel • blowdryer • brush • comb • curling iron • hair spray • jawclips

1 Rub a small dollop of gel through damp hair, then flip head upside down and blow-dry. When hair is dry, flip head back up and lightly brush. Use a comb to give yourself a center part.

2 When the curling iron is hot, wrap a small section of hair around the barrel. Only curl up to ear level—the top should stay straight. Clamp the iron closed and leave for 5 seconds. Release. Repeat on the rest of your head.

3 Spritz your head with hair spray, then pull the front back and clip behind your ears. Be sure to attach the clips right at the beginning of the curls, so hair is smooth above them.

style tip

If your hair is super-curly, you can skip the curling iron entirely. Instead, start with damp hair and apply gel from the roots and halfway down, and then smooth the hair down with a comb. Pin the hair securely behind your ears with combs to keep it smooth even longer.

dress it up!

This clip can just be slipped in and will hold hair securely behind your ears.

A comb is another alternative to hold hair in place.

A cluster of small barrettes like this one works just as well as one big clip.

clip it back!

To give this look an even more glamorous and romantic feel, try pulling the front section back loosely and securing it with a pretty clip in the back. Make sure the clip sits low to keep the loose style.

thetwist

First we showed you what a cool idea it is to twist up the front of your hair. Now imagine if you added two twisted pigtails to the mix. That's right, your head is totally twisted! Depending on the accessories you choose, you can take this style from subtle to far out just by changing the jawclips or adding a flower accessory. We love this style because it looks complicated, but once you master it, you'll be able to bust out the Twist in just a few minutes.

how to do it

you'll need: wide-tooth comb • 3 medium jawclips • 6 mini jawclips • hair elastics • bobby pins • hair spray

1 Start by combing hair straight back with a wide-tooth comb. Use the comb to create three sections (left, center, and right) and secure each with a medium jawclip. Now remove the medium-size clip from one of the sections, and pick up about half of the width of this section at the hairline. Start twisting the piece back with your fingers, picking up the hair directly behind it as you go. Secure the twist with a mini jawclip.

2 Continue twisting sections until all three big jawclips are replaced with cute twists. Next, divide the loose ends between two low pigtails in the back, and secure with elastics.

3 Grab one pigtail and twist it until it coils around the elastic. Pin it with bobby pins to hold in place. Do the same to the other side, then spritz head with hair spray and pat down any stray hairs.

dress it up!

Twist-in gems are a great way to dress up the two twisted buns in back!

Mini tortoiseshell clips hold twists in place and look great on all hair colors.

Beaded hairpins dress up your twists with a bit of glitz.

style tip

Girls with bangs can do this style in a couple of ways: twist bangs back with the rest of your hair, or let them hang loose.

wraparound

These over-the-head braids are totally hip—and cute to boot! They're also so easy to do (after you master the art of braiding) that you may just find yourself sporting this look Monday through Sunday. You can use accessories to make it right for anything your week may hold.

style tip

If your hair is super-long, you might be able to loop the braids back and forth over your head. Just tuck the ends under wherever they land.

how to do it

you'll need: brush • comb • hair elastics • bobby pins

1 Brush dry hair to remove any tangles and, using a comb, divide your hair into two equal sections (left and right).

2 Grab the right section of your hair and start braiding (for details on how to braid hair, see Low Braids on page 34). Be sure not to make braids too tight—starting about an inch down from the scalp will help. Do the left side the same way.

3 Lift both braids up and secure them at the top of your head using bobby pins. Tuck the ends under to make it look like you've got one smooth braid going around.

dress it up!

Use a bejeweled bobby pin to attach the braids at the top of your head.

This flower pin would look great slipped into one of the braids right above your ear.

Position this butterfly bobby to peek out from under braids for a playful touch.

Twist these hair gems into the braids for some nighttime drama.

glamourwaves

You may think that hot rollers are for grandmothers only, but learning to curl your hair makes it easy to create lots of new styles—including simple but glamorous waves. These glamour waves look great on everyone, and can be worked into an updo and dressed up for a party, or hang down for a fun day of shopping.

how to do it

you'll need: spray gel • wide-tooth comb
• rollers (with pins) • hair spray

1 Lightly spray damp hair with a spray gel from roots to ends. Use a wide-tooth comb to get rid of tangles and distribute the gel evenly. Give yourself a center part using the comb. Next, grab a two-inch- (5-cm-) square section of hair on the right side of the part and comb it out again.

2 Grab a hot roller and place it underneath the ends of the section. Start rolling toward your scalp. When the roller reaches your scalp, secure it with a roller pin. (Unless you have self-sticking Velcro rollers, the pins should be included.) Repeat until all hair is rolled up.

3 Leave curlers in for about ten minutes, or until they are cool. (If you're using Velcro rollers, use your blowdryer to heat the curls.) Remove all the rollers and run your fingers through hair to loosen the curls into pretty waves. Spritz with hair spray to give your curls extra staying power.

style tip

If your hair is fine and stick-straight, spritz the piece of hair that you're about to put in the roller with hair spray beforehand to make sure the curl sticks.

dress it up!

A fancy headband in hot pink and silver sets off this pretty style.

Rhinestones make this barrette a dressed-up way to pull curls back for a special occasion.

Flowery bobby pins are great for keeping hair out of your face in style.

Try a dark-colored clip to blend in with brown or black hair in the prettiest way.

crimpedandcool

Are you ready to make waves? If you've never tried this funky style before, then get set to have some fun. Not only is the whole look of crimped hair super-cool, but it's also a great thing to do with friends. Why not have some of your girlfriends come over during the day and get out the crimping iron? You'll have a wild style for going out to the movies or to a party.

how to do it

you'll need: leave-in conditioner • blowdryer • paddle brush • crimping iron

1 Start by spritzing damp hair with leave-in conditioner from roots to ends to help to protect it while you are crimping. Next, flip head upside down and blow-dry. When hair is dry, brush it to remove any tangles. Plug in your crimping iron to let it warm up.

2 Hold up a small piece of hair and clamp the crimping iron around it, near the roots. Leave the crimping iron closed for 3–5 seconds, then release. Move the crimper down the hair so the top is just below where the last crimp ended. Be sure to hold the crimper in place for the same amount of time in each place.

3 When you have crimped your whole head, lightly brush hair once to create a full effect. Spritz your whole head with hair spray to help the crimp last as long as you can.

dress it up!

These bobby pins are great for adding a little color right near your face.

Wear a couple of these clips in a row and add some serious style.

This skinny headband is perfect for pulling out-of-control hair back.

style tip

If you have bangs, either pull them back in this style or just skip the crimp. Crimped bangs look totally weird!

These silver jawclips sparkle with rhinestones.

clip it up!

Crimped hair can get B-I-G, so if it's falling in your face, it's a good idea to clip the front sections back. Start by making a center part that ends in the middle of the top of your forehead. Grab a small section of hair from one side and twist it three times before pinning it back a couple of inches (5–6 cm). Do the same with the other side.

What's your best look for special occasions?

Do you have a go-to hairstyle for weddings and dances? What do you do with your 'do for a holiday dinner? Which accessories look best when it's time to get really glammed-up? Need a bit of inspiration? Look no further! This section has party-perfect hair covered—with tons of cascading curls, sophisticated twists, sparkly hair accessories, and even chopsticks (trust us, they look seriously cool). Some of these styles are trickier than others, but even girls who can't tell a curling iron from a crimper will find lots of looks that are totally do-able—and totally chic. Plus, you'll find tips on getting creative to make each look unique. So what are you waiting for? It's time to party!

Nierah

ponytailwrap

Got a last minute party invite? Whip up this polished look in a flash. While some glam hairdo's take a while to master, this pretty pony can literally be done in minutes. You can keep it chic and simple or add a little sparkle with your favorite hair accessory. A sparkly bobby pin would look pretty slipped in your hair right at the temples, but some cool dangling earrings will also do the trick.

how to do it

you'll need: paddle brush • hair elastic • bobby pin

1 Start by brushing your hair and then scooping it back into a low ponytail, leaving a small section of hair from underneath the pony out of the elastic.

2 Wrap the loose section of hair around the elastic until there is only a one-inch section left. Secure the end underneath the ponytail with a bobby pin.

why not double up?

If one ponytail wrap is good, then two are positively fabulous! Just divide hair into pigtails instead of a pony in Step 1. For a cool, futuristic look, try using a bigger piece of hair as the wraparound.

change it up!

style tip

Hey, fine-haired girls: to avoid taking volume away from your pony, keep the wraparound piece pretty skinny. You can also use mousse to plump up your hair before pulling it back in Step 1.

dress it up!

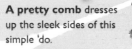

This bobby pin with a star pattern will look great sweeping aside grown-out bangs.

This rounded barrette does the wraparound look in an ultra-glittery way.

A pretty comb dresses up the sleek sides of this simple 'do.

These twist-in rhinestones will look great in darker hair.

fliptail

A gorgeous party style that only takes a hairbrush and hair elastic? It does exist! This style is so simple you'll wonder why you didn't think of it before. But just because it's easy to master, don't think it's boring. With a few key accessories, you can transform it from spunky to romantic to drop-dead gorgeous!

how to do it

you'll need: hairbrush • hair elastic

1 Start by brushing dry hair straight back and securing it into a low ponytail with an elastic. Don't have the elastic right at your scalp; make the pony a little loose.

2 Use your fingers to make a hole in the hair directly above the elastic (this is why you want it loose).

3 Hold the hole open with one hand while the other hand flips the ponytail under and up through the hole. Smooth hair into place with your hands, and you're done!

romantic flip

Girls with curly or thick hair can go for this graceful look by keeping the flipped-under ponytail very low and loose. You can also pull out some pieces of hair from the front to frame your face and really up the pretty factor.

change it up!

This leather band is ideal for a low ponytail. The stick slides through to keep it in place.

dress it up!

An elastic with rhinestones adds a party flair to hair.

This leather butterfly looks perfect in curly hair.

Colorful bobby pins sweep back loose pieces and give this style extra flare.

A beaded hairpin adds sparkle. Just stick it right at the ponytail holder to accent the feature flip.

style tip

Girls with straight hair can add a little pizzazz to the Flip Tail by curling the ends of the ponytail with a curling iron.

perfectpompadour

Don't you love this look? We think it's super-cool because it looks totally 1950's yet modern. Teasing is one of those hair tricks that was massive a few years ago and has now made a comeback. Not only is this look mega-glam, it's also flattering to most faces since it adds volume at the top of your head. Go on—grab your comb and be a tease!

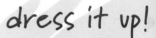

dress it up!

A glittery jawclip will hold thick hair in place.

how to do it

you'll need: blowdryer • hair elastic • fine-tooth or teasing comb • bobby pins • hair spray

1 Start with damp hair. Flip your head upside down and blow-dry while scrunching with your hands—don't use a hairbrush. When hair is dry, flip head rightside up and smooth with your fingers.

2 Gather the side and back of your hair into a loose ponytail that sits in the middle of the back of your head. Leave the top of hair loose.

3 Take the front of hair and hold it straight up. With the other hand, place the teeth of the comb at the top of the hair, then drag it to the roots (this is called teasing). Do this a couple of times, then repeat on the rest of the loose section.

4 Next, gather all of the teased sections and pull them back toward the crown of your head. Twist the hair around your finger to create a loose coil. Pin the coil at the crown.

5 Use your fingers to gently lift the hair up at the front (this gives you the pompadour part). When you've pulled it as high as you want to go, lightly comb the top smooth and mist your whole head with hair spray to keep it in place.

This elastic is a glam option for securing finer hair.

Add this barrette right behind the pompadour to keep it pouffy and in place.

hang loose!

The pompadour looks equally good on its own, so feel free to skip the pony in the back and just leave your hair hanging down.

This elastic with a butterfly attached looks perfect in this pompadour.

style tip

Girls with curls can skip the teasing steps because with all those ringlets you've already got tons of volume. Lucky you!

ponytailveil

If you love to wear your hair down but still want to add a little personality, this style is for you. This latticework 'do looks sleek from the front and beyond pretty from the back. And don't be afraid to glam the veil up even more with hair gems—they add dressy sparkle when placed at the elastics or anywhere along the sections of hair.

how to do it

you'll need: hairbrush • 6 hair elastics

1 Brush dry hair backward until it's really smooth. Pull the top-center section back and secure with an elastic band. Gather the hair in front of your ears on the left side of your head in an elastic. Do the same with the right side. You should end up with three separate sections of hair in an arc of elastic bands over the crown (and across the back) of your head.

style tip

If you have fine hair, try topping off each elastic with a jawclip so the veil doesn't slip.

2 Divide the center ponytail into two sections and connect the right section to the right ponytail using a small elastic. This elastic should sit about two inches (5 cm) below the first elastic.

3 Take the left section of the middle ponytail and connect it to the left ponytail. You will now have two ponytails hanging down. Finally, connect both ponytails into one.

dress it up!

Pick up some small jawclips in a color that matches your outfit.

This textured elastic is great option for girls with fine hair as it will really hold the tiny ponytails in place.

These jeweled hairpins will work right above each elastic for a little shimmer.

These small sparkly combs will look lovely slipped in right above one of the top ponytails.

Hair gems can be twisted into hair in between the elastics for added glamour.

These hair jewels snap on like buttons.

frenchbraid

When it comes to French Braids it seems like everyone falls into one of two categories: those can do them and those who can't. If you haven't learned them yet, we've got you covered with the step-by-step on a style that's never out of fashion! The reason we love French Braids is that once you've got them in, they stay put. They're absolutely perfect for a family wedding or anything else that's fun but formal.

style tip

If you want to let your bangs hang loose, just start the braids a little farther back on your head.

how to do it

you'll need: hairbrush • wide-tooth comb • 2 hair elastics

1 Start with dry hair. First, brush to remove any tangles. Make a middle part from the front of your hair all the way to the back using a wide-tooth comb. Secure one side with an elastic to get it out of the way for now.

2 Working with the loose side, grab the hair from the front of your head and separate it into three sections. Start by crossing over the sections once, like you would a normal braid (check out Low Braids on page 34 for instructions).

3 Before crossing the right side to center again, pick up a piece of hair from outside of the braid so that it becomes part of the righthand section. Then cross the combined section over to center.

4 Next, grab a small piece of hair to the left of the braid and add it to the lefthand section. Cross the combined left section over to center.

5 Keep braiding like this—adding in hair before every cross—until all the loose hair is incorporated into the braid. Continue to the end of your hair with a regular braid and then secure with an elastic. Do the same with the opposite side.

dress it up!

This shiny bauble wraps up braids with a splash of fun.

Why use a plain elastic when you can use this bejeweled one?

Use mini-clips to pull back shorter pieces that won't stay put in the braid.

Don't you love these colorful and crinkly elastics?

change it up!

Leave the ends loose to make this style more casual—just stop once you've French braided down to the hairline and secure hair with a cute ponytail holder. You could also stop the braid partway (use a barrette to hold) and let the bottom half of your hair fall free for a pretty half-up/half-down version.

braidybun

If you've ever spent time in ballet classes, you'll know that this style is perfectly pretty and easy to do. The trick to making this kind of bun flattering is to do it high enough so that you can see it from the front. When a style is as simple and sleek as this one, the only real way to give it personality is with hair accessories, so don't hold back! Twist in some gems or slip in a comb— call on color and sparkle for pizzazz.

how to do it

you'll need: brush • hair elastic • bobby pins

1 Brush dry hair to make sure it's knot-free. Gather all of hair up into a high ponytail and secure with an elastic.

funky bun

See these gems in her hair? So pretty

After you've put your hair up in a ponytail, why not create lots of tiny braids instead of one big one? Just braid as many little ones as you want, then wrap the whole collection around and pin it in place. You can also try twisting the whole bunch first or leaving some loose for different variations on this 'do.

change it up!

dress it up!

This pink comb will look great slid next to the bun so the teeth point toward its center.

Clip these rhinestones right underneath the bun.

Twisty hair gems look fab circling the bun—or in any configuration you can think of!

style tip

Curly girls should start with damp hair to make this style look extra sleek.

2 Divide the ponytail into three sections. Begin braiding by crossing the righthand section over the middle section and then the lefthand section over the middle section. Repeat until you reach the end of your hair.

3 Wrap the braid around the elastic and tuck the end of the braid under the bun. Slide in a bobby pin to secure it. Pin the rest of the braidy bun in place by inserting bobby pins all around the base of your bun until it feels secure.

elegantupdo

Remember the movie about the girl who nobody noticed in school—then suddenly she meets the perfect guy and he takes her to the prom? Well, this is the hairstyle she's wearing as she walks into the dance. And, could there be a more perfect hairstyle to show off a few girly hair accessories? You can pull from our ideas and go for bold and sparkling, or pluck a flower from the garden as your au-natural accessory. Now that's fresh!

how to do it

you'll need: paddle brush • hair elastic • hair spray • bobby pins • curling iron

1   First, plug in your curling iron. Start the style by brushing dry hair backward and securing it with an elastic into a high ponytail. Separate out a section of your ponytail—about one sixth of your hair.

2   Spritz the small section with hair spray and wrap it around your finger to create a loose coil. Then use a bobby pin it to pin the coil to the base of the ponytail.

style tip

Not everyone's hair holds a curl the same. If your's isn't as curly as you want after five seconds, roll it up in the curling iron again and hold for another five seconds.

3   Separate another small section right next to the pinned-up piece. Spritz with hair spray to get it ready to curl. Then open the curling iron and wrap the hair around the barrel. Close the iron and hold for five seconds. Spritz with hair spray again to help set the curl.

4   Alternate between pinning coiled sections down and curling sections until the entire ponytail is done. If you want more curly tendrils, you can curl the sections around your face as well. At the end, spritz your whole head with one final mist of hair spray.

dress it up!

Small sparkly twists pack a big glam impact tucked between loops.

This bejeweled pin would look fab stuck in right next to the ponytail.

This butterfly elastic loops around your ponytail to give you glitz from the get-go!

A pretty comb pushed underneath the bun gives a ballerina look.

change it up!

up in a bun

For a gorgeous variation of this updo, skip Step 3 and repeat Step 2 until all the pieces of your ponytail are looped and pinned like the first. You can create an even more intricate look by using smaller pieces of the ponytail. Be sure to choose occasion-appropriate accessories to complete the look.

simply**beautiful**

◔◰ This style is truly fit for a princess. It's chic, classic, and the perfect 'do to show off a fabulous barrette. Since this look is all about learning how to do a pro-quality blow-out, it might take a couple of tries to master. Trying to hold a blowdryer in one hand and the brush in the other may feel a little awkward at first, but after a while it will become second nature—and you'll look Simply Beautiful!

how to do it

you'll need: straightening balm or cream
• wide-tooth comb • 6 jawclips • blowdryer
• round brush • shine spray • paddle brush • barrette

1 Start with damp hair. Massage a quarter-sized dollop of straightening cream through hair from roots to ends. Comb hair to remove tangles, then use the comb to make a side part from the crown of your head forward. Divide hair into six sections (three top and three bottom), twisting and clamping each section with a jawclip.

2 Section by section, begin blow-drying hair. Use a round brush on the underside of the section, pulling it down from roots to tips with the hairdryer blowing right above it. Repeat this on every section until hair is smooth and dry.

3 Spritz hair with shine spray and brush. Grab a section from the front (a little smaller than the width of your forehead) and pull straight back. Use a paddle brush to brush it really smooth, then clip the section a couple of inches (about 5 cm) back.

dress it up!

This tortoiseshell barrette is perfect if you want to sport this style at school.

A pretty comb is a great option for holding back fine hair.

This rhinestone clip is an easy way to add some glitter to your look.

style tip

If your hair is kinky curly, save yourself the muscle power. It takes a professional to blow-dry real ringlets straight.

add some curls

If you've got straight hair, it looks pure pretty to add some curls to the ends of your hair with this style. (Follow Step 3 from the Elegant Updo on page 82 to master the curling iron.) When you're done, spritz your hair with hair spray to make sure your new curls last.

pick-upsticks

Look totally original (and utterly hip) by putting chopsticks to a new use. This crafty style adds Asian flair to your hair with delicious results! Stick dressed-up sticks into an already cute bun for a look that's perfect for going to a friend's birthday party or out on the town.

how to do it

you'll need: brush • hair elastic
• bobby pins • pomade • hair sticks

1 Start by brushing dry hair to get rid of any tangles.

2 Flip your head upside down and pull your hair into a high ponytail. Secure with an elastic.

3 Twist the ponytail into a tight coil, then twist it around the elastic to create a bun. Secure the bun with plenty of bobby pins. (But make sure to leave a few ends sprouting out!)

4 To finish your look, rub some pomade into the sprouty ends so that it looks a little piece-y. Stick two sticks in an X formation into the bun.

dress it up!

These sticks that are touched with gold are perfect for a dressy occasion.

Sticks in bright pink will work on any hair shade.

These wavy sticks will look great on blondes or redheads because of their dark color.

style tip

Hair too short for an all-out bun? Try doing a mini-bun with the top half of your hair. Just use smaller sticks so they don't overpower your 'do.

frenchtwist

The French Twist is a total classic—always glamorous and beautiful. But just because this is a timeless technique doesn't mean your 'do will look stuck in the Dark Ages. What keeps our version modern and absolutely fabulous is its funky loosened-up look. Let hair stick out of the top in a cute sprout, pull some loose pieces down to frame your face, and voila! Beautiful.

how to do it

you'll need: hair spray • bobby pins • pomade

1 Lightly mist dry hair with hair spray before gathering it in the back of your head as if you were going to do a low ponytail.

2 Start twisting the hair while pulling it upward at the same time (the ends of your hair should be pointing to the ceiling). Keep coiling until only the ends of your hair are sprouting out.

3 Insert bobby pins all the way up the coil to hold everything in place.

4 Pull front sections of hair down to frame the face. Warm a pea-sized amount of pomade in your fingers and rub it onto the "sprout" to make it really piece-y.

long and loose

Instead of the sprout, try winding ends around to make a loose bun at the top of the twist. This modification looks great with curls— pull a few out of the back and sides for a super-romantic mystique.

Use a glam bobby pin to put curls just where you want them.

style tip

Girls with thicker hair look great in this style. Just be sure to use lots of bobby pins to keep everything in a twist!

dress it up!

Insert this butterfly hairpin right above the updo.

Use a rhinestone barrette to clip back any stray front sections.

With a giant jawclip, this style goes from glamorous to casual.

sleeksidebun

When is a bun not a bun? When it kicks to the side for a whole new take on sleek! This style is super-flattering because from the front, you'll see the bun poking out from one side—so it's a little less severe than the regular kind. Plus, this is a simple way to change a hairstyle that you may already know how to do but didn't know how to update.

how to do it

you'll need: brush • wide-tooth comb • hair elastic • bobby pins • shine spray

1 Brush dry hair to remove tangles. Use a wide-tooth comb to create a side part. Gather your hair into a low ponytail on the opposite side of the part.

change it up!

This flower pin will stay secure if you push the teeth of it into the bun.

make it messy

You can also take this style and make it look a bit more edgy by following the steps for a Messy Pony on page 22, then coming back to Sleek Side Bun for Steps 2 and 3.

style tip

Got curls? Make the bun a little looser for a softer style—or add some shine spray before you twist up into the sleeker version.

dress it up!

A shimmery comb can tuck right into the top of the bun.

This barrette-and-bun coverup combo will make you look pretty in pink.

Rows of rhinestones will light up your look! Try a pair of these for special occasions.

2 Twist the ponytail tightly until it starts to coil up, then wind it loosely into a bun. Secure the bun by sticking in bobby pins from all sides of the bun (if you feel them cross over, that's great because your hair will really stay in place).

3 Lightly mist your whole head with a shine spray and clip in a hair decoration with some sparkle.

curlycue

Looking for a style that's perfect for a party but still loose and carefree? This is it. Romantic ringlets falling over your shoulders are a little bohemian but still super-pretty. Plus, who doesn't like to change the texture of her hair? It's fun to try ringlets—and with the right curling iron and a little hair spray you'll be good to go!

how to do it

you'll need: spray gel • comb • rollers (with pins) • hair spray • hair elastic • bobby pins • curling iron

1 Start by curling hair into Glamour Waves by following the instructions on page 64. When you're done, create a side part with a comb.

2 Gather the top of hair at the crown of your head and twist it into a loose coil. Place a few bobby pins to hold the coil in place, but leave some pieces loose.

3 Do the same to the bottom half of hair, so there are two coils, one above the other.

4 To finish the look, use lots of decorative hair accessories to pin the curls where you want them. Be sure to leave a couple of pieces loose to frame your face.

hippie chick

Give this romantic style more of a bohemian look by adding some baby braids (see Braid Crazy on page 36) randomly throughout the style. Secure them with tiny elastics or jawclips.

Be bold with bright mini jawclips.

dress it up!

Stick this flower pin in your hair so it looks like it's tucked behind your ear.

A bobby pin with a dangling jewel will look lovely clipping up a curl.

style tip

Straight-haired girls will definitely want to use a curling iron on the sections around your face.

glossary

Blowdryer: A styling tool that uses hot, pressured air to dry, and, with the aid of a round brush, to straighten hair. Some models also have a cold setting that blasts cool air to set curls.

Bobby Pins: Metal pins used to hold pieces of hair tightly in place or help hold an updo securely. Available in different colors to blend in with various hair colors, or with decoration such as gems or flowers.

Brush (paddle): A brush that has a flat top with bristles on one side. Best used for brushing out tangles on dry hair.

Brush (round): A brush that has bristles all the way around the top. Best used for blowing hair straight or curling the ends of your hair.

Chignon: A French term for a classic type of updo. It's always at the back of your head is a very smooth and sleek version of a bun.

Comb (fine-tooth): A usually plastic styling tool with very small teeth set close together; best for finishing touches like smoothing down stray hairs or making a precise part.

Comb (wide-tooth): This kind of comb has big gaps between the teeth, which makes it ideal for combing damp hair.

Conditioner (leave-in): A light cream or spray added to damp hair after showering. Great for dry hair, and also as a protective layer before using heated styling tools.

Conditioner (regular): A creamy moisturizing product used after shampoo. Can be applied to full hair shaft of normal hair, or just to ends of oily hair.

Crimping Iron: A V-shaped styling tool with two metal plates that create a zig-zag form when clamped together. Used to create a frizzy style.

Crown: The top-back part of your head, where a center part begins. This is a flattering place to put high ponytails and buns, since you can see the style from the front and the back.

Curling Iron: A barrel-shaped heated styling tool that hair wraps around to set in a curl. Available in small, medium, and large widths for tight or loose curls.

Flatiron: A heated styling tool that uses two flat metal plates to iron hair straight.

French Twist: A classic style in which hair is pulled back, twisted upward, and pinned in place.

Gel: A sticky styling product that works best to add volume to roots or hold hair in place for a complicated updo. Best applied to damp hair for firm hold.

Hairpins: Metal styling pins shaped like a narrow U for securing loose pieces of hair in updos. Available in natural colors to blend into hair.

Hair Spray (aerosol): A dry styling product that comes in a can and is sprayed on in a fine mist to give hair a final hold after styling.

Hair Spray (pump): A wet styling product that is sprayed onto hair in a mist. Best used with heated styling aids, which will dry the spray for extra holding power.

Mousse: A light, creamy styling aid with drying ingredients, great for creating lift. Best applied near roots with fingers or a wide-tooth comb.

Pomade: A semi-hard, waxy styling aid that usually comes in a flat tin. It's best used on the ends of hair to make it look piece-y or textured.

Pompadour: A '50s-style hairdo in which the front is combed back into a pouf and the sides and back are slick.

Rollers (hot): Heated styling aids that come on a base with metal heating rods sticking out. The rods heat the rollers, which can then be fixed in hair with pins to set soft curls.

Rollers (Velcro): Non-heated rollers with Velcro teeth to hold their place in hair without pins. A blowdryer is needed to heat and set the style.

Scrunching: A way to add volume and texture to hair by balling up a handful of hair and squeezing it with your fingers.

Shampoo: A cleansing product for hair. Should be used every day or every other day in a formula designed for your hair type.

Straightening Cream or Balm: A lotion-like styling product applied before using a blowdryer or other heated styling aid to protect hair against heat damage.

Teasing: A technique for adding pouffy volume to hair. A fine-tooth comb is used to brush hair backward into loose tangles.

Wax: A hard styling product similar to pomade but less greasy. Good for making ends piece-y or adding definition and separation to ringlets.

index

Acknowledgments

The publisher would like to thank the following for their kind cooperation in the preparation and production of this book:

Our fabulous models:
Sakura Akiyama-Bowden, Brittany Barbone, Andrea Bloom, Tess Brokaw, Amy Cacciatore, Alexis Carmody, Michelle Chionchio, Mary-Kate Duffy, Kelsey Evenson, Rosie Fodera, Hannah Gross, Nierah Jinwright, Sade Johnson, Maghee Kelsall, Sade Johnson, Juliette Lam, Nikki Lam, Francesca Lobbe, Juliana Merola, Kristin Molinari, and Autumn Stiles…and also their parents, who stuck with us so very patiently at the photo shoot.

The amazing hairstylists:
Azad Desmeropian, Shukran Dogan, Catherine McDermott, Rhondalyn Roberts, John Lisa, and Angela Woodley, for their wonderful skill and dedication.

The super stylists: Maria Stefania Vavylopoulou and Shima Green, for outfitting the girls in the coolest clothes.

Special thanks to Vincent DeRosa and Suzanne Humbert at Whisper Soft Mills for the beautiful bedding and furnishings.

Thanks also to Josephine and Katherine Yam and the team at Colourscan for their hard work in bringing it all together; to Nanette Cardon for her work on the index; and of course to the always-glamorous Angela Coppola, Donna Mancini, Cristina Clemente, Nichole Morford, Sharon Lucas, and Gregor Hall for all their help and support.

Hair products used in this book included these products from the L'Oréal Studio Line: Crystal Wax, Out of Bed Whipped Gel, Mega Mousse, Mega Gel, Fast Forward, and Finishing Spray.